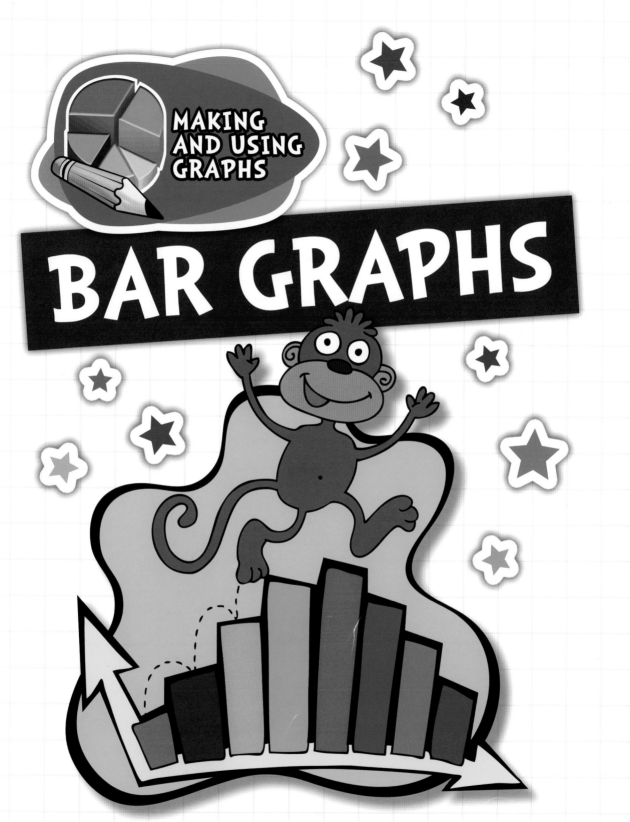

MAKING AND USING GRAPHS

BAR GRAPHS

by Lisa Colozza Cocca   illustrated by Kathleen Petelinsek

CHERRY LAKE Publishing

Published in the United States of America by Cherry Lake Publishing
Ann Arbor, Michigan
www.cherrylakepublishing.com

Consultants: Janice Bradley, PhD, Mathematically Connected Communities, New Mexico State University; Marla Conn, Read-Ability

Editorial direction: Rebecca Rowell
Book design and illustration: The Design Lab

Photo credits: Kristian Sekulic/iStockphoto, 4; Shutterstock Images, 8; Uyen Le/iStockphoto, 12; Doug Berry/iStockphoto, 16; Bart Coenders/iStockphoto, 20

Library of Congress Cataloging-in-Publication Data
Cocca, Lisa Colozza, 1957–
  Bar graphs / Lisa Colozza Cocca.
      pages cm. — (Making and using graphs)
  Includes bibliographical references and index.
  ISBN 978-1-61080-911-5 (hardback : alk. paper) — ISBN 978-1-61080-936-8 (paperback : alk. paper) — ISBN 978-1-61080-961-0 (ebook) — ISBN 978-1-61080-986-3 (hosted ebook)
1. Graphic methods—Juvenile literature. 2. Mathematics–Charts, diagrams, etc.—Juvenile literature. 3. Mathematical statistics—Graphic methods—Juvenile literature. I. Title.

  QA90.C57 2013
  001.4'226—dc23
                                    2012030944

Cherry Lake Publishing would like to acknowledge the work of The Partnership for 21st Century Skills.
Please visit www.21stcenturyskills.org for more information.

Printed in the United States of America
Corporate Graphics Inc.
January 2013
CLFA10

Table of Contents

CHAPTER ONE

What Is a Bar Graph?

A bar graph can show how many boys and girls are in a class.

Are there things you want to count and compare? A **bar** graph can help. It's a type of number picture. A bar graph can show if your class has more girls or more boys.

Bar graphs can also show how things change over time. A bar graph can show you how much you've grown. Do you want to know more about bar graphs? Let's go!

A bar graph has many parts:

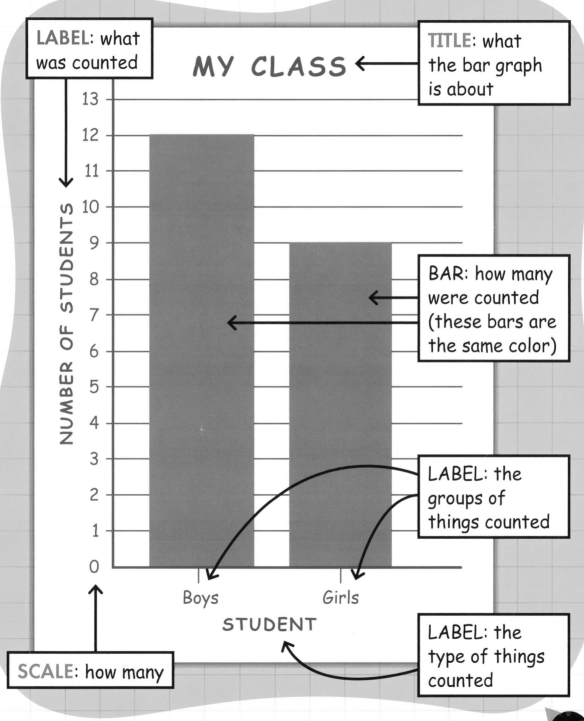

LABEL: what was counted

TITLE: what the bar graph is about

MY CLASS

BAR: how many were counted (these bars are the same color)

LABEL: the groups of things counted

NUMBER OF STUDENTS

Boys

Girls

STUDENT

LABEL: the type of things counted

SCALE: how many

Bar graphs can have all kinds of colors.

A bar graph uses bars, or rectangles, to show amounts. Each bar stands for **data**. In some bar graphs, the bars are **vertical**. They go from bottom to top. In other bar graphs, the bars are **horizontal**. They go from side to side. The bars in a graph can be the same color, different colors, or different patterns.

What kinds of things can we graph? Let's find out!

Here's what you'll need to complete the activities in this book:

- notebook paper
- pencil with an eraser
- ruler
- crayons or markers

Gather what you need.

CHAPTER TWO

Graphing Balloons

You're invited! Let's count things for the party.

Let's have a party! There are all kinds of things we can count and compare.

We have balloons for the party. We can make a bar graph to compare how many of each color we have. First, we can make a **tally chart**. To tally is to count. Use a tally chart to track what you count. This is a great way to collect data for our graph.

PARTY BALLOONS

COLOR	NUMBER	TOTAL
Blue	‖‖	4
Red	⫲⫲⫲ ‖	7
Yellow	‖‖	3

We'll track the balloon data in a tally chart.

The colors of our balloons are listed at the left. Each color has its own row. We make a **tally mark**, or line, for each balloon we count. The fifth mark goes across the other four.

Next, we count the tally marks in each row. We write the numbers in the chart.

Now, let's make a bar graph. We'll use vertical bars. The names of the colors go across the bottom. Each color will have a bar. We write numbers along the side. The data from our tally chart tells us how many balloons of each color we have. That tells us how tall to make the bars.

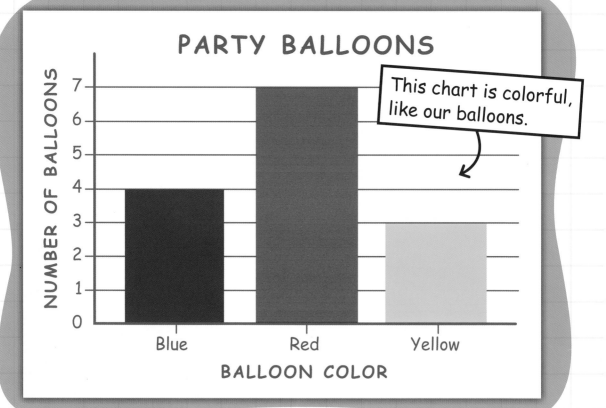

Our bar graph shows there were more red balloons than blue. What else does it show? How many yellow balloons were there?

Graph Car Colors

Practice making a vertical bar graph. Compare the cars on your block.

INSTRUCTIONS:

1. Use the tally chart on page 9 as a model for your chart.
2. Count the different colors of cars on the block where you live. Fill in the chart as you count.
3. Make a vertical bar graph with your data. If you need it, use your ruler to make straight lines. If you want, make each bar a different color.
4. Label the parts of your graph. Remember, the numbers go along the side. The car colors go along the bottom.
5. Give your graph a title.
6. Tell a parent what your bar graph shows.

To get a copy of this activity, visit www.cherrylakepublishing.com/activities.

CHAPTER THREE

Graphing Food

We're having fruit salad at our party.

We need food for the party. Let's make fruit salad! We have apples, bananas, oranges, and strawberries. Let's count how many pieces we have of each type of fruit. We can compare the amounts in a bar graph.

We collected our data in a tally chart. It shows how many pieces of each fruit we have. Let's make a bar graph using this data.

FRUIT SALAD		
FRUIT	PIECES	TOTAL
Apples	|||||		6
Bananas	||||	4
Oranges	||||	4
Strawberries	||||| |||||	10

We have lots of fruit for our salad.

Let's use horizontal bars this time. The names of the fruits go along the side. The numbers go along the bottom.

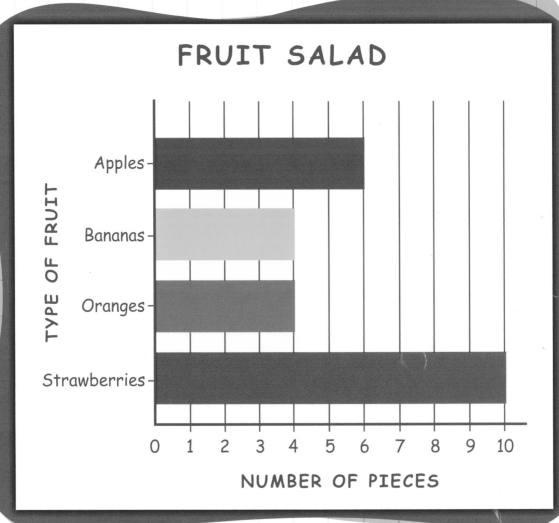

FRUIT SALAD

TYPE OF FRUIT

Apples
Bananas
Oranges
Strawberries

0 1 2 3 4 5 6 7 8 9 10

NUMBER OF PIECES

Our bar graph shows many things. How many apples do we have? Do we have more bananas or oranges?

Graph Fruits or Vegetables

Practice making a horizontal bar graph. Compare fruits or vegetables you have in your kitchen.

INSTRUCTIONS:
1. Use the tally chart on page 13 as a model for your chart.
2. Count the fruits or vegetables. Fill in the chart as you count.
3. Make a horizontal bar graph with your data. If you need it, use your ruler to make straight lines.
4. Draw bars using your data. If you want, make each bar a different color.
5. Label the parts of your graph. Remember, the names of the fruits or vegetables go along the side. The numbers go along the bottom.
6. Give your graph a title.
7. Tell a friend what your bar graph shows.

To get a copy of this activity, visit www.cherrylakepublishing.com/activities.

CHAPTER FOUR

Graphing Guests

It's time for the party. It's scheduled from 1:00 p.m. to 3:00 p.m. Guests arrive at different times. We can make a bar graph to show how the number of guests changes over time.

It's party time! Let's count guests.

PARTY GUESTS	
TIME	NUMBER
1:00 p.m.	1
1:30 p.m.	8
2:00 p.m.	12
2:30 p.m.	10
3:00 p.m.	6

First, let's make a chart of our data. The times when we count go on the left side. The numbers of guests we count go on the right side. This time, instead of using tally marks, we just use numbers.

Let's graph our data. We'll make a vertical bar graph. The times go along the bottom. The number of guests goes along the side.

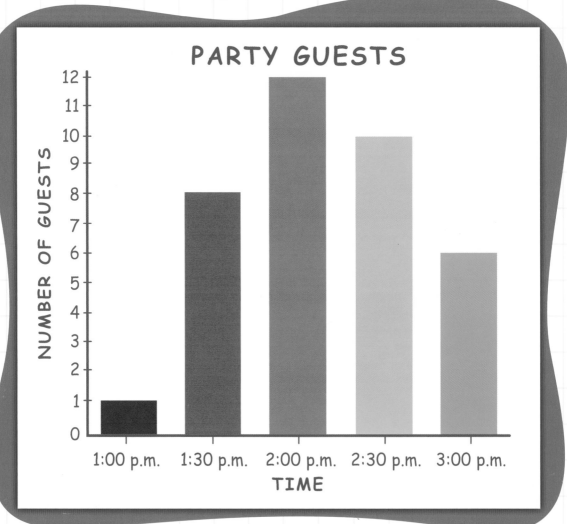

At what time did we count the most guests? How many more guests were there at 1:30 p.m. than at 1:00 p.m.?

Graph People

Practice making a bar graph showing change over time. Count the number of people you see in a park or other public place every 15 minutes for one hour.

INSTRUCTIONS:
1. Use the chart on page 17 as a model for your chart. Count the number of people you see every 15 minutes. Fill in your chart as you count.
2. Make a vertical bar graph with your data. If you need it, use your ruler to make straight lines.
3. Draw bars using your data.
4. Label your graph. Remember, the times go along the bottom. The number of people goes along the side.
5. Give your graph a title.
6. Tell a teacher what your bar graph shows.

To get a copy of this activity, visit www.cherrylakepublishing.com/activities.

MONKEY PARK

CHAPTER FIVE

Bar Graphs Are Fun

Parties are fun. Bar graphs are fun, too.

Bar graphs are a fun way to show data. Bar graphs are a fun way to learn, too. They help us understand things. We can use them to compare the numbers of things. And we can see how something changes over time.

What else can you compare with a bar graph? Keep practicing!

Here are some fun new ways you can use bar graphs:

- Compare the numbers of birds you see by color.
- Compare how many hits a baseball team makes each inning.
- Measure a puddle every few hours. Show how the size of the puddle changed.
- Plant seeds. Once your plants start growing, choose one and measure it each week. Record your data. Show how your plant grew over time.

Practice counting and comparing using bar graphs.

Glossary

bar (bahr) a rectangle or stripe

data (DAY-tuh) information recorded about people or things

horizontal (hor-i-ZAHN-tuhl) going straight across or side to side

label (LAY-buhl) a name

scale (skale) a series of numbers that shows how many

tally chart (TAL-ee chahrt) a way to record things you count that uses tally marks

tally mark (TAL-ee mahrk) a line that stands for one item of something being counted

title (TYE-tuhl) the name of a chart

vertical (VUR-ti-kuhl) going straight up and down

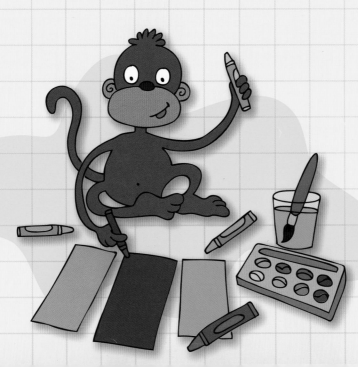

For More Information

BOOKS

Bader, Bonnie. *Graphs*. New York: Grosset & Dunlap, 2003.

Leedy, Loreen. *The Great Graph Contest*. New York: Holiday House, 2005.

Murphy, Stuart. *Lemonade for Sale*. New York: HarperCollins, 1998.

WEB SITES

BrainPOP Jr.—Tally Charts and Bar Graphs
www.brainpopjr.com/math/data/tallychartsandbargraphs/
Watch a fun video about making a tally chart and using it to make a bar graph.

Kids' Zone: Learning with NCES—Create a Graph Classic, Bar Graph
nces.ed.gov/nceskids/graphing/classic/bar.asp
Build a bar graph by filling in the labels and data. One click turns your data into a bar graph.

Math Is Fun—Make a Bar Graph
www.mathisfun.com/data/bar-graph.html
Build a bar graph by adding your own labels and data. Make the bars one color or many colors.

Index

About the Author

Lisa Colozza Cocca is a former teacher and school librarian. For the past decade, she has worked as a freelance writer and editor. She lives, works, and plays in New Jersey. Lisa thinks graphs are lots of fun.